Dear Future

Thanks to the Year 6
students from Laburnum.
Good luck in the future!
Thanks also to Katherine
Neuendorf and Arlene Liew.

Written by Meredith Costain
Illustrated by Teresa Culkin-Lawrence
Designed by Peter Shaw and Sarn Potter

Published by Mimosa Publications Pty Ltd
PO Box 779, Hawthorn 3122, Australia
© 1995 Mimosa Publications Pty Ltd

Literacy 2000 is a Trademark registered in the
United States Patent and Trademark Office.

Distributed in the United States of America by
RIGBY
A Division of Reed Elsevier Inc.
PO Box 797
Crystal Lake, IL 60039-0797
800-822-8661

Distributed in Canada by
GINN PUBLISHING CANADA INC.
3771 Victoria Park Avenue
Scarborough
Ontario M1W 2P9

99 98 97 96 95
10 9 8 7 6 5 4 3 2 1
Printed in Hong Kong through Bookbuilders Ltd

ISBN 0 7327 1575 X

Dear Future

MEREDITH COSTAIN

Illustrated by
Teresa Culkin-Lawrence

This is me!

Hi. I'm Anna. Anna Loredana Eugenia Hope Reynard to be exact. It's a bit of a mouthful, I suppose, but all those extra names in the middle help to keep the grandmothers and great-aunts in my family happy. With a name as long as that, you'd expect me to be tall. I'm not. If anything, I'm on the short side. And I've got thick, wavy dark hair (from the Anna Loredana side) and brown eyes (from the Eugenia Hope side). I'm almost eleven, and I go to school here in Chinchilla.

I like school. Well, most parts of it, anyway. I like reading and writing stories best, and learning about other people and places. And I love doing special projects. Our whole class does. Maybe that's because of our teacher, Ms. O'Shane.

On Friday Ms. O'Shane came into class with a special smile on her face. Ms. O'Shane has lots of different smiles. We've seen this one before. It means we're going to start a new project. A fun project, she said. When Ms. O'Shane describes a new class project, she's always really enthusiastic. She stands up there in front of us flapping her arms about and doing dramatic head gestures as she speaks. By the end of it, her amazing mane of red hair looks as though she's been in a high speed car chase in an open-topped car. Sometimes I think she likes doing the projects even more than we do.

Ms. O'Shane in action

We've done some pretty weird projects so far. Once we built a space station out of cardboard and foil and old cans and stuff. We used different sized balls for the planets – a tennis ball for Jupiter and a marble for Pluto, and a bouncy little ping-pong ball for Earth. Another time we kept a spider called Frederick Peabody in a fishtank (after we'd taken the water out, of course!), and studied his behavior. Until he escaped. That was a bit scary, especially for Ms. O'Shane. Perhaps she was afraid Frederick would get caught up in her hair and never leave. We eventually found him tootling across an orange in the principal's fruit bowl. After that we decided he was probably safer out in the wilderness.

Fred the Spider

But this new project sounded pretty amazing. It got us all thinking, that was for sure. Really thinking.

"We're going to make a time capsule," Ms. O'Shane enthused.

Nobody was quite sure what that was.

"Is it something for the space station?" asked Luis. "So the people can travel around?"

"Is it like a time machine?" asked Ling Ling. "So we can visit the future?"

Ms. O'Shane smiled. "No," she said, "but it has got something to do with the future. A time capsule," she went on, "is like a record of a period in history. And we're going to show people in the future what it was like to live now – what our suburbs are like, what our school is like, anything we can think of that the Futurites might like to know. Everyone in the class can think of something."

We'd put everything in a big box, seal it up in plastic, write the date on it, then bury it in the schoolyard. And we'd put a big notice on it that said, NOT TO BE OPENED FOR ONE HUNDRED YEARS.

Well, we all loved the idea. I found myself thinking about how neat it would be to find the capsule. Imagine looking into a big box full of things from a hundred years ago! You probably wouldn't even recognize some of them.

Of course everybody had different ideas about what they'd like to put in the time capsule. Some kids, like Jordan, came up with

Jordan's crazy idea!

really dumb ideas, like putting whole cars and television sets in. Imagine burying a whole car in the schoolyard! Even if the yard was big enough, we'd still need to hire some kind of earth-moving equipment to dig the hole. Ms. O'Shane patiently explained that we wouldn't have enough room to put in such large objects. But we could include models, she said, or we could draw up posters that showed what things looked like now and how they worked.

I thought for ages about what I was going to do. I wanted to do something really different. Something special. But I just couldn't think of anything. I decided to talk to Nonna about it when I got home from school. Nonna is my grandmother (on the Anna Loredana side). Her name is Anna, too, and she's kind of short, like me! She lives with us. Mom and Dad are still at work when my brother Marco and I get home from school, so Nonna looks after us.

My Nonna

Nonna had a great idea. She knows how much I enjoy writing. She said that the best thing I could do was write about what my life is like now, so that kids in the future could compare it with theirs. You know, just little everyday things, like what I do on the weekend when I'm having fun with my friends, and what I eat for breakfast, and what books I like to read. Maybe the person who reads it will also be someone who likes finding out about other people and places. Wouldn't that be great!

Nonna told me that we know more about certain times in history because some people in the past kept journals – like Samuel Pepys and Anne Frank. Nonna's read both their journals.

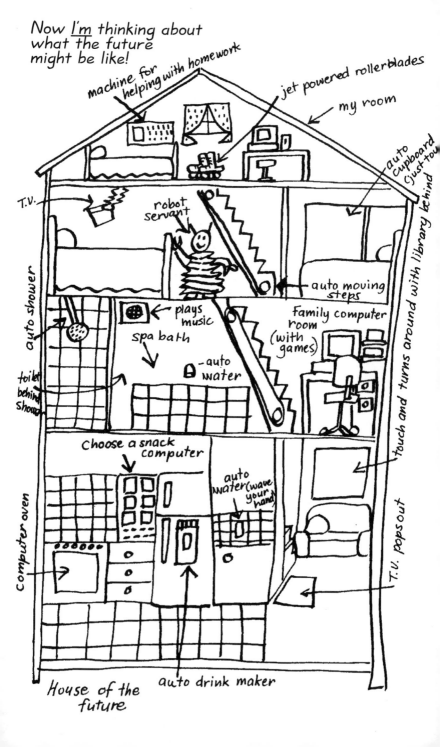

She's always reading. She reads more books than everybody else in our family put together. Every Saturday morning, she goes to the local library and raids their shelves, and sometimes I go and help. Marco hates reading. He'd much rather play computer games. Well, I like them too, but books are still my favorite.

But that got me thinking. What if in a hundred years time everybody used computers all the time? Even now we can look up things on a computer just as though it were an encyclopedia. And sometimes we can use computers to learn about history and spelling and things, rather than from Ms. O'Shane. What if everything was on computer in the future, and there were no more books at all?

So then I decided to write a journal, as Nonna had suggested, in a really nice book. Maybe, in one hundred years time, it would be the only book around . . .

Tuesday, April 15

Dear Future,

This morning everybody in my class came into school buzzing about what they were going to do for their projects for the time capsule. Some kids are working in pairs. A few kids have already started bringing in really complicated and expensive-looking materials. But not me. I'm just going to sit here quietly and write to you, because for my contribution to our class project I'm going to keep a journal. That way I can tell you about lots of different things – things that happen to my family, my classmates, and me over the next few weeks. I hope you will enjoy reading it, and that you will learn something about what it was like to live in our time.

I used some of my birthday money to buy this really nice book from the newsdealer's. I hope its pages are still smooth and creamy when you get to read it, and that its leathery brown cover looks as nice as it does now. But the best thing about it is its smell. It smells just like a book. Sort of papery and gluey and leathery. Do your books smell like that? Do you even have books, or is all your information on computer? Nonna (my grandmother) has loaned me her special fountain pen to write with. I hope the ink won't have faded by the time you read it.

This is my Mom!

It was my birthday last week. I turned eleven. Legs eleven, my dad said. I had a big chocolate cake with candles, and a special dinner – minestrone and lasagne. My favorites! And my best friend Allyson came. I wanted to have a party, but Mom said maybe next year. I can't wait!

Nonna

Marco

I got some great presents – clothes and books, and a big box of chocolates. My little brother, Marco, is really cute. He gave me a black jellybean. It had been in his pocket for ages and was all covered in fluff. I put it in the garbage, but I made sure that he wasn't looking because I didn't want to hurt his feelings. Marco loves black jellybeans and he's probably been saving it specially for me, trying really hard not to eat it. Well, he's only five. It's pretty hard to have self-control at that age.

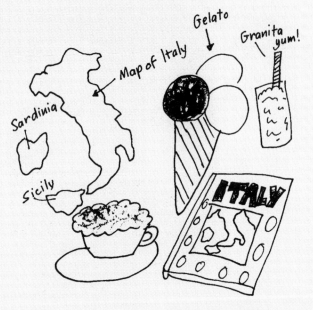

Gelato

Granita
yum!

Map of Italy

Sardinia

Sicily

ITALY

Nonna gave me a book with photos in it of her village in Italy. Nonna is Italian and so is my mother. My father isn't, so that makes me only half Italian. I can speak some Italian, but not very well. The writing in the book is in Italian and I asked Nonna if she'd read it to me. She said she would, after she'd had a little rest. Nonna's been pretty tired lately; in fact, I don't think I've ever seen her look so tired. I hope she's okay. I took her a cool drink, and played with Marco at the other end of the house so he wouldn't disturb her while she was sleeping.

Ms. O'Shane came into class this morning carrying a cardboard box so big that we could only see her legs and the top of her bushy red hair behind it. It said FRAGILE in large letters on one side, and THIS WAY UP. But she wasn't carrying it the right way up at all, and she was bumping it all over the place. If there had been anything inside, it would have been lucky to survive that. Carlos asked her if it was going to be the time capsule box, but she just shook her head and looked mysterious. I wonder what it's for?

Anna

TRANSPORT

by Sa

ROAD

Motor Bike

This is a

1000 c

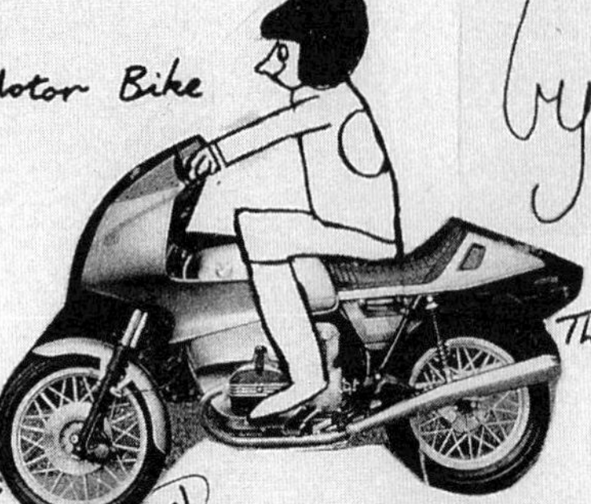

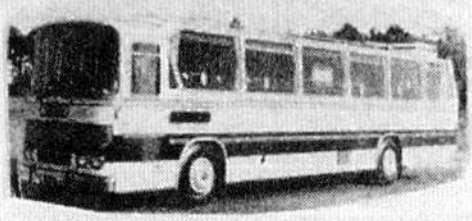

I go to school by bus.

HOW MY CLASS GETS TO SCHOOL:

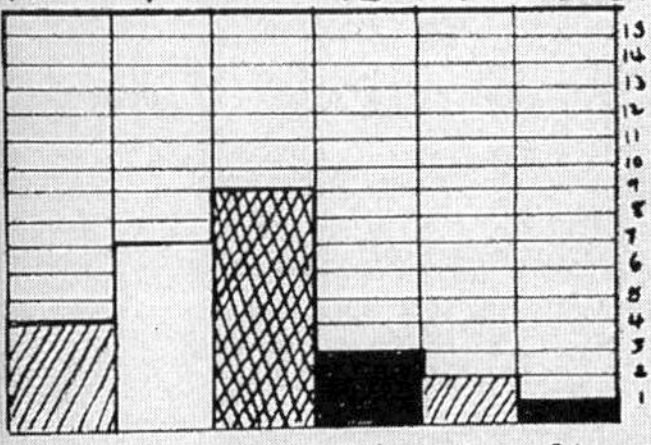

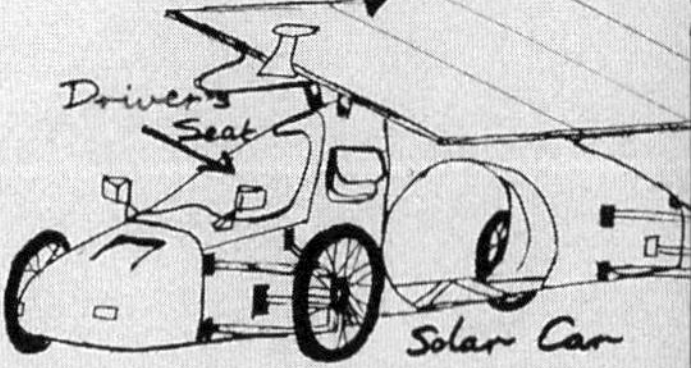

15
14
13
12
11
10
9
8
7
6
5
4
3
2
1
Car Bus Walk Bike Train Skateboard!

wheee!

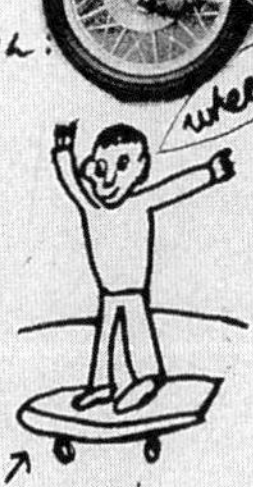

Solar Collector
Driver's Seat

Solar Car

SEA

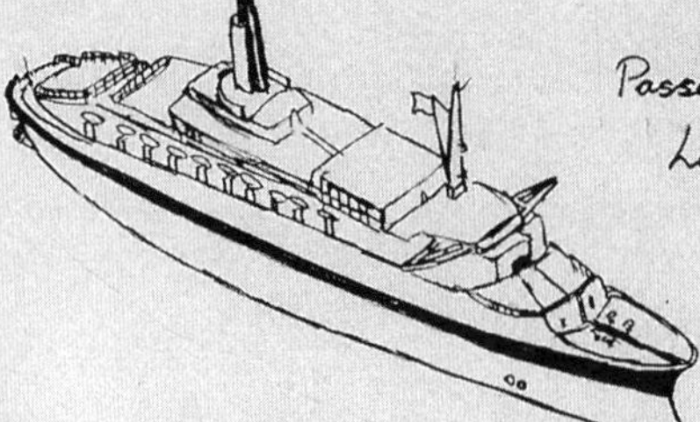

Passenger Liner

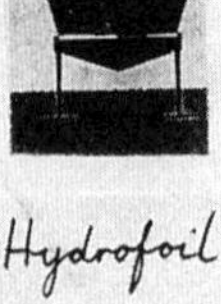

Hydrofoil

Driven by powerful pumps

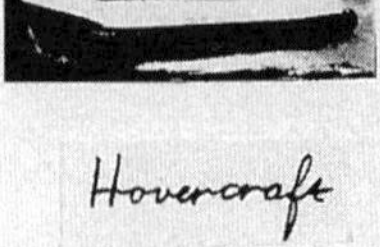

Hovercraft

Rides on a cushion of air

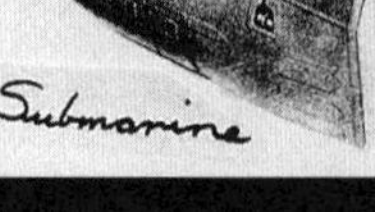

Submarine

(Goes under the sea)

This is how we travel around in the 20th Century!

RAIL

Monorail (only one track)

Some passenger trains can carry up to 500 people at one time!

How trains switch tracks

Guardrail

Crossing

Point

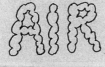
AIR

Some different kinds of aircraft:

This plane is faster than the speed of sound!

Helicopter

FORCES ACTING ON AN AIRPLANE:

Lift

Drag

Thrust

Gravity

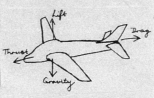

Passenger Plane

Rocket

Wednesday, April 16

Dear Future,

    It's just as well Ms. O'Shane has given us a few weeks to do our projects for the time capsule, because lots of really exciting things are going to be happening at the same time. Today Mr. Polette, our drama teacher, announced that we're going to have a school concert! It will be held in the school hall, and we're going to have a real audience and programs and ticket-sellers – the works!

    But first we're going to have auditions. That means that everyone who wants to be in the concert has to try out their act first in front of Mr. Polette and his assistant, Ms. Rubinstein; then they'll choose the final line-up.

    I'd think I'd like to be in the concert, but I'm not sure if I could get up in front of all those people. What if I made a mistake, or got stage fright and forgot my act halfway through? I've never been very good at doing things in front of other people; I get really jittery. When I was in

Grade 2, I played the part of a goose in our class play. (It was the story of Henny Penny, so there were lots of parts for birds.) But my big beaky mask was too big and fell over my eyes. I couldn't see a thing and walked right off the edge of the stage. It wasn't very high, and I didn't hurt myself badly or anything, but everyone in the audience absolutely howled with laughter. It was so embarrassing!

How embarrassing!

Me as a goose!

I'd like to do something, though. I'll talk it over with Nonna tonight, so long as she's not too tired. She's still looking pale, and she's been having more and more rests. In the mornings, her eyes are puffy and red, as though she's been crying. Last night I asked her if anything was wrong, and she patted my hand and told me not to worry. But I do worry. She's my nonna and I love her. I don't want her to be tired and unhappy.

Ms. O'Shane came into class with something else strange today: wire mesh. What could she possibly be going to do with that?

Jasmine decided to do her project on our class's favorite foods. She asked everyone to bring in their favorite recipe. Goran got mixed up and brought in a slice of real pizza, with double cheese and anchovies. Imagine what that would have smelled like by the time you came across it in a hundred years. Peeeyewwww!

Anna

gooey double cheese

anchovies

24

Jasmine's Project

Josh: champion cook!

Our class is full of food lovers. Here are the recipes for some of our favorite dishes. I wonder if you'll still be able to get all the ingredients in one hundred years' time.

Spaghetti Bolognese

1 pound of minced steak
1 tablespoon oil
2 onions, chopped
1 clove garlic, crushed
1 can tomatoes
1 tablespoon tomato paste
1 cup water
black pepper
mixed herbs
parmesan cheese

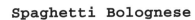

Fry onion and garlic in oil until light brown.
Add meat and brown well.
Add rest of ingredients and simmer for at least one hour
Serve over spaghetti.
Sprinkle with parmesan cheese.

Chocolate Cake

1 cup self-raising flour
1 cup sugar
2 tablespoons cocoa
2 eggs
1/2 cup milk
dash vanilla
2 tablespoons butter

Melt butter and pour over combined ingredients.

Mix everything together well and bake for 50 minutes at 350°F.

THE CHOCOLATE CAKE
(a Poem by Jasmine)

I love to make
A chocolate cake -
It only takes an hour,
Even though
From head to toe
I get covered up with flour!
I love to bake
A chocolate cake
It's really rich and yummy;
Here's some advice -
Too big a slice
Can upset your tummy!

Fried Rice

3 cups cooked rice
3 slices ham, chopped
1 tablespoon oil
1 onion, chopped
1 cup bean shoots
2 eggs beaten
2 shallots, chopped
2 tablespoons soy sauce

Fry onion and ham in oil.
Add bean shoots.
Add rice and fry until lightly
browned.
Add soy sauce and beaten eggs.
Stir well.
Cook for one minute.
Garnish with shallots and serve.

Bon appetit
and buen apetito!

I asked my school class and friends:

Food	most liked
Spaghetti	15
Chocolate Cake	8
Fried rice	7
Pizza	2
Peanut butter sandwiches	1

Dear Future,

I didn't have time to write to you yesterday – we were all too busy working out our acts for the school concert. There are lots of talented people in my class! Sharon and Suzie are really good at singing. They're going to do a rap about our school that they wrote themselves. It's wicked*! Just like the songs real rappers do. Ms. O'Shane said it was so good that they

should put the words in the time capsule, to show you what our music was like.

* Some of the words in fashion at the moment have totally different meanings from the way they're normally used. "Wicked" means really good, amazing, cool. (Oops, there I go again!)
Do you have words like this too?

Carlos has transformed himself into a magician, Carlo the Magnificent! He's got a top hat and a swirling black cape and a wand! He spent nearly all day practicing a trick he does with rings and scarves, so

CARLO the MAGNIFICENT.

that he'd do especially well at the audition. But then tragedy struck. During lunch hour, Thumper, his pet rabbit that he pulls out of his top hat, escaped from his box. We all helped him look for Thumper, but he was just nowhere to be found. Poor Carlos was heart-broken. He said that Thumper was the best part of his act.

A whole lot of the really sporty ones are getting together to do a gymnastics display. I'm not really good at tumbling or cartwheels or anything, though. It's not really my sort of thing, if you know what I mean. Actually, I haven't worked out what I'll do for the audition yet. I will soon, though.

I was going to discuss it with Nonna again last night because she always has such good ideas. And she always seems to know what to say, especially when you're feeling a bit downhearted.

But last night it was Nonna who was feeling bad. And I finally found out why. Nonna is sick. Not just some little thing like a cold or stomach upset that will go away in a few days. I mean seriously sick. She's going to have to go into hospital next week for some tests. She told me not to worry, and that I had to be strong for her. She said that if she knew I was being strong while she was in hospital, she wouldn't have to worry about me and Marco while she wasn't there to look after us. That's so like Nonna. Always thinking of others, never herself.

We sat together on her big, high bed. It's got a beautiful quilt embroidered all over with sunflowers. She says they remind her of the sunflowers that grew in the fields around her village in Italy. Then she started to read the book to me, the book with the pictures of her village. She said she'd read me a little bit every night until she went into hospital. And when she came out, if we hadn't finished it, she'd read me the rest. My throat got all lumpy and hot and my eyes went prickly when she said that, but I was determined not to cry.

Oh! I nearly forgot. Ms. O'Shane came into school today carrying a blob of green slime. Not real slime — it's imitation plastic stuff you can buy in trick shops for playing jokes on people. Carlos once put a piece of it in Jasmine's pencil case. When she opened it and her fingers touched the icky, knobbly surface she threw it up in the air and screamed so loudly that the teacher in the next room came running in to see what was wrong. Mr. Hendrix, our teacher last year, confiscated "the blob" so that Carlos couldn't try it on anyone else. I guess it's still sliming around in his top drawer.

Everyone laughed and held their noses when Ms. O'Shane brought the slime in, as though we thought it was real slime. We thought we'd just go along with whatever trick she was trying to play on us. But she just walked straight to the back of the room and put it in her special cupboard, near the window. There's a notice on that cupboard that says NO PEEKING ALLOWED. Everybody's dying to know what she's got in there, but I guess we'll never find out, because it's got a huge padlock on it. Very mysterious.

Anna

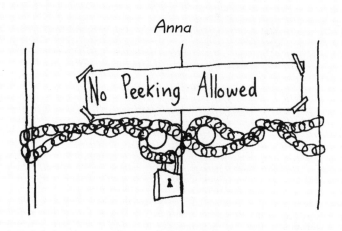

The Cool School
by Sharon & Suzie

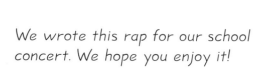

We wrote this rap for our school concert. We hope you enjoy it!

The Chinchilla School Rap

Listen up people
Got a song about a school
Going to tell you the story
Of a school that's cool

Cool – Chinchilla
Our school – Chinchilla

On our block
Is a building made of brick
Where the kids learn
Spelling and arithmetic . . .

Cool – Chinchilla
Our school – Chinchilla

Now in this school
Is a spider named Fred
Who ran riot for a week
Just looking to be fed

Cool – Chinchilla
Our school – Chinchilla

Our teacher's name
Is Ms. O'Shane
And she's so cool
That we never complain

Cool – Chinchilla
Our school – Chinchilla

Now Ms. O'Shane
Has a mane of red hair
But we searched in vain
For the spider there!

Cool – Chinchilla
Our school – Chinchilla

And in our room
Is a tank full of fish
When they swim and play
Their tails go swish!

Cool – Chinchilla
Our school – Chinchilla

We love Chinchilla
We'll never swap
And we'll keep on rapping
Till it's time to stop

Cool – Chinchilla
Our school – Chinchilla

We'll be in the concert
That's for sure
And we'll do this rap
For a big encore!

Cool – Chinchilla
Our school – Chinchilla
Cool - Chinchilla
Our school - Chinchilla!

Monday, April 21

Dear Future,

　　Well, I'm back at school and writing in my journal after the weekend. On Saturday morning Mom took Marco and me shopping. She wanted to get Nonna a new dressing-gown and some slippers, to wear in hospital. We helped her choose some really nice, soft blue slippers and a long, warm dressing-gown. I knew Nonna would like the gown because it has beautiful golden sunflowers embroidered on the collar. And I could tell that I was right by the way her eyes shone softly when we gave it to her. Then she gave us all a big hug.

The stores were full of all the latest clothes. There are so many different styles. What kind of things do you wear? Maybe you'll have invented some sort of crushproof, wrinkle-free cloth that never gets dirty! My parents would love that. They hate doing the washing and ironing.

While we were at the mall we watched a dog-training demonstration that a pet food company was putting on. Most of the dogs carried out their trainers' commands perfectly. They fetched and carried and did all kinds of special tricks. One could even walk on two legs! There was one dog, though, a little black poodle named Dolly, who was having trouble. She just sat there, looking nervously around her, giving little yips. It's almost like she had stage-fright. She looked so sad. Her ears hung down and her eyes seemed to be saying, "I'm trying, but I'm really scared with all these people watching me." I wanted to pick her up and take her home. I know just how she felt. It is hard getting up in front of lots of people.

At school sometimes, if we've written an especially good story, Ms. O'Shane asks us to stand up in front of the class and read it aloud. Well, I love writing stories, but whenever this reading part comes along, my knees start shaking and my throat goes scratchy and dry. It's not that I don't want other people to know what I've written. And it's a nice feeling when other people enjoy your work. I'm just a bit shy, I guess.

That's why it's good having a journal to write in. I can write down all the things I do and feel (like what I just told you about being shy). And even though I know that someone (you!) will eventually read it, it's not as if you know me. I'm just a girl who lived one hundred years before you. It's kind of weird, isn't it! But nice weird.

I have to stop writing now. Mr. Polette has come to talk to us about the concert. I still haven't worked out anything to do yet. But I'll think of something, I know I will; hopefully something that doesn't involve having to get up on that stage!

Oh, yes. Ms. O'Shane is still bringing in strange things. This morning she came in with a bucket full of sand – just plain old sand, like Marco's got in his sandbox at home. She walked in really casually with the bucket, as if it was something she carries around every day, and put it down beside the mystery cupboard at the back of the room. She could see all our mouths gaping open, but she wasn't about to tell us a thing! Curiouser and curiouser, as Alice in Wonderland would say.

Anna

ROBBIE'S PROJECT

These are the clothes that many kids like to wear. They're cool and radical! How do they compare with yours?

WINTER CLOTHES

SUMMER
CLOTHES

45

Tuesday, April 22

Dear Future,

   I didn't have time to work out an act for the concert last night. Mom wanted me to help Dad make supper and read Marco his bedtime story, while she was helping Nonna get ready to go into hospital tomorrow.

   After Marco had gone to sleep I went into Nonna's room so she could read me the next bit of the Italian book. We snuggled up together under her sunflower quilt.

Nonna and me
reading a book

She read me the part about the mountains near her village, and how in winter their tops are always covered in snow. Her eyes looked misty as she read that bit. I asked her if she missed her village, and she squeezed my hand and said yes, she did sometimes. But she was very happy with her new home here, with us.

I saw her looking at the suitcase on the floor near the door, all packed and ready for hospital. I wanted to ask her if she was worried about what might happen

to her while she was in there – what the tests might show. I think she knew what I was thinking. She always does, somehow. Maybe it's because we've got the same name. She squeezed my hand again, extra hard this time. Sometimes, you don't need words.

Before I went to bed, I gave Nonna a special photo of our family that I keep by my bed. It's in an old silver frame that my mom was given when she was a girl, and that she gave to me. The photo was taken last year, when we all went to the beach for summer vacation. Dad's messing around making silly faces and hugging Mom. Marco is building a huge sand castle. Nonna and I are holding hands. It's a nice photo. I feel good knowing that Nonna can look at the photo if she ever feels sad or nervous about being in hospital. I hope it will help her remember how much we all love her.

Today some of the kids showed us their acts for the concert. The song that Sharon and Suzie wrote is really witty. I'm sure they'll get picked. Duc, Sam and Mehmet have worked out a play based on the superheroes from adventure movies.

The whole class found it so
funny that we almost hurt from laughing,
and they had amazing costumes. Duc even
had a rubber sword which wiggled around
all over the place when he
waved it heroically in
the air. Ms. O'Shane
asked me if my act
was ready yet, and
I told her that it
was – nearly.
I just needed a
little more
time.

She looked at me with her head on one side. She had dinosaur earrings on, and the T-Rex one wobbled when it hit her shoulder. I looked at it rather than into her eyes, because I knew if she looked into my eyes she would know that I didn't have an act at all.

She asked me if there was anything I wanted to talk to her about, or if she could help me in any way. She asked me in a really quiet voice, so that no one else could hear. I told her that everything was fine – mostly. But then I admitted that I was a bit worried about performing in front of a lot of people, in case I clammed up and forgot my act, or accidentally fell off the stage. She didn't even laugh when I said that, even though I knew she'd been in the audience when I did my goose bit that time. Ms. O'Shane is nice like that. She said she'd put her thinking cap on and try to come up with something for me to do where there was no danger of being anywhere near the edge of a stage. I went to lunch feeling as though six big rocks had been lifted off my shoulders.

At lunchtime Allyson and I learned a new way of playing hopscotch. It's called snail hopscotch. Do you still play hopscotch? It's been around for hundreds of years already, so maybe you do. You draw up a series of squares with a stick or piece of chalk, then hop in and out of the squares, kicking your stone. In this new game, the squares curl around and around, just like a snail. Right in the middle is the "home" square, where you can put both feet down. I was really glad when I reached home – it's hard work doing all that hopping! I'll draw you a picture of the court so you can play too.

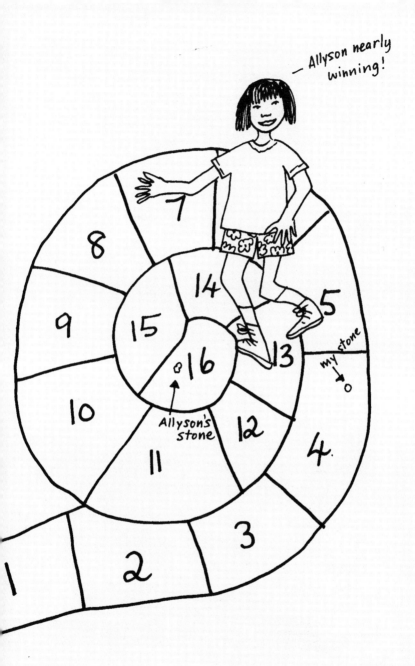

53

What sort of games do you play?
Here at school there's always a craze on
for one game or another. Last year it was
elastics. That was fun. Every recess and
lunchtime, you'd see kids jumping in and out

My Aunt Anna
Plays the piano
Twenty-four hours a day.
Pepper!

of elastic loops wrapped around other kids'
ankles. Then we had a jump-rope craze.
We'd all line up and jump in and out of
twirling ropes while we chanted jump-
rope songs. Here are some of my favorites:

Texaco, Texaco,
Over the hills to Mexico,
Turn around, around, around
Get out of town, town,
town.

We play lots of marbles, too. Allyson
has an enormous marble. She's beaten
everyone in the class with it – even
Mehmet, who used to be the school
champion at marbles until Allyson came
along. It's green and yellow and looks just
like a big cat's eye.

And sometimes we play chasing
games. Snake tag's my favorite.
When you get caught you have
to join onto a big line and
conga your way around
the playground.

Ms. O'Shane came into class today with a special surprise — popsicles for everyone! We all clapped and cheered and told her she was the best teacher ever. She said there was a special condition, though. When we'd finished eating the popsicles, we had to give her the sticks. And if we ate any more during the week, she wanted us to collect the sticks and give them to her. I wonder what she could possibly want to do with them all.

Anna

Carla's Project

Dear people of the 21st century,

My name is Carla and I love collecting things. I've got special display cases and shelves in my bedroom that show off all my collections.
These are some of the things I collect:

Chickens

Magnets

Toys

Shells

Coins

Stamps

I also love anything to do with cats. These are some of the cat things that I have collected:

three cat coffee mugs
ten books about cats
four cat calendars
one cat scarf
twenty-seven cat cards
three stuffed toy cats
a set of cat coasters
one cat address book
one special cat plate
eight pottery cats (including one large one)
one cat teapot
one cat pin
...and a photo of my cat, Harley!

I collect cats because they are
Cute
Amiable
Tranquil
Slinky

... Carla

Cats

61

Friday, April 25

Dear Future,

   Today was audition day! Everyone
went over to the hall and sat on the
benches, waiting to do their acts. Mr.
Polette and Ms. Rubinstein sat in the
front row with clipboards and lists and
called out names. Suddenly it all seemed
very professional. We all got to watch the
acts while we were waiting.

   I've already told you that there are
lots of talented kids in our class. But at
the auditions I realized there are talented
kids all over the school. It was going to be
really difficult to choose between them.
Lots of kids played musical instruments,
but the best one was a really tiny girl
with small round glasses and freckles,
Melissa Armitage. She came onto the
stage lugging a big black case that looked
like it might have an elephant in it. It was
just about bigger than her! We thought it
might have something to do with Carlo the
Magnificent's magic act, but no. She
unlatched the hinges and produced an

enormous, shiny silver thing — a euphonium.
Then she sat down on a chair (we could
just see her behind the euphonium) and
began to play "Moon River." I think she
made a few mistakes, and she ran out of
breath a few times, but it was really
impressive.

Arnold Shepherd recited one of his poems, of course. This one was called "Tragedy on the High Seas." Arnold's always writing poems and entering them in competitions. They're ... well, interesting, and long. His mother is an actress, and she's been coaching him in how to project his voice and do dramatic hand gestures. He'd asked for the lights to be turned down, with only the small one above him still on. He looked like a traffic officer directing cars in the main street, at night. He was wearing a long red chiffon scarf tied around his neck, and a few times his hand gestures got a bit caught up in it. Some kids sniggered, until Mr. Polette turned around and gave them one of his withering looks. That soon stopped them.

A withering look

64

The worst act was the boys from Grade 6 who played trumpets. They were meant to be playing jazz, but their unstructured approach sounded more like a troop of sick cows. Everybody put their hands over their ears, except Mr. Polette who is always keen to encourage even the slightest talent. I somehow don't think they're going to be chosen for the concert.

When it came to our class's turn, everybody except me went up to the stage. Ms. O'Shane came and sat next to me while the gymnastics display was on. She said that she and Mr. Polette had found a special job for me to do – a very important job.

Nonna in hospital

They want me to organize and design the program for the concert. She said they need a very special person who is good at writing. Wow! Ms. O'Shane thinks I'm good at writing! I felt really, really proud. I can't wait to tell Nonna when we go to visit her in the hospital tonight.

We've been to visit Nonna every night this week. She's in a nice ward with other old ladies. There are lots of flowers and cards everywhere which is good, because everything is so white in there – white walls, white floors, white sheets. It must be hard keeping everything so clean. There's an old lady in the bed next to Nonna's. She's so small she hardly takes up any room in it. I don't think she gets many visitors. Well, I haven't seen any. Her name's Mrs. MacDougall, but all the nurses call her Mrs. Mac. I decided I would visit her as well as Nonna when I go into the hospital. That way she mightn't feel so lonely. Maybe I'll take her some flowers tonight as well. Her bedside table looks kind of empty.

Anna

Juliana's Project

What is your school like? I've collected some clippings about things that have happened at our school this year and put them together in a special scrapbook. Happy reading!

CHINCHILLA STUDENTS IN DISTRICT ATHLETICS COMPETITION

Four students from Chinchilla School, Sally O'Hearn, Rocco Manetto, Mariam Yousef and Ling Ling Ho, have all won places in the Southside District athletics competition.

Sally took out first place in the Under 10 100 yards against strong competition. Rocco soared over the bar to trounce the opposition in the Under 9 high jump. Both these students also performed creditably in the long jump.

Mariam came second in the Under 8 100 yards, and Ling Ling took out third place in Under 11 hurdles.

Their trainer, Ms. Alicia Fury, was thrilled with their performances, and is looking forward to the State finals in September.

ALL AT SEA

Parents and friends of students at Chinchilla School were treated to a performance of "A Life at Sea," the latest production by the school's drama department.

Directed by Mr. Pierre Polette, the cast included students from every level in the school. Pirates, mermaids, sailors, fish, and singing parrots provided a delightful evening's entertainment.

The sets were painted by the students themselves, under the eye of art teacher Ms. Rita Da Costa, and costumes were made by parents of the students in the play.

TREEPLANTING AT CHINCHILLA

Students from Chinchilla School gathered last week to plant a line of trees along the western side of the school.

Helped by their principal, Ms. Poulos, and their teacher, Ms. O'Shane, the students spent last Wednesday morning digging holes for the ten native saplings.

"It will help make the school grounds more attractive and entice native birds to the area," explained Ms. O'Shane. "The students will take turns watering the trees and keeping records of feathered newcomers to the area."

The saplings were provided by Greenfingers Garden Center, as a gift to the school.

GRANDPARENTS' DAY

Last Wednesday was Grandparents' Day at Chinchilla School. Students were invited to bring their grandparents along for the day to see them at work and play.

Some grandparents gave talks about what life was like in their day, while others were happy simply to sit and watch lessons. Refreshments, provided by the students, were served with morning coffee. The school band performed for the school's special visitors at lunchtime.

Thursday, May 1

Dear Future,

I haven't written to you for the last few days because I've been so busy. I've been working on the program for the school concert. I talked to all the performers and took notes, so that I could write a short description of each act. I want it to be a really good program, and I don't want to let Ms. O'Shane down.

I've also been really worried about Nonna. We go to visit her every night at the hospital, and she always looks so pale, lying there in that big, white hospital bed. She's had her tests now, and Mom told me yesterday that she has to have an operation - a serious one.

I burst into tears. Mom was crying too. We stood and hugged each other for ages, slowly rocking together. Marco came in and wanted to know what the matter was. Then Dad came along and carried him away on top of his shoulders. It's hard to explain about illness and operations to someone who's only five.

Later that night, while I was sitting in my room with my Italian book, I thought about what hospitals might be like in your time. Maybe scientists will have invented all sorts of wonder cures by then. Or maybe they'll be able to stop sick people from feeling any pain. I wished I could invent something that would help Nonna. And then I thought of it. I'd take her sunflower quilt into the hospital. I know that it reminds her of her village in Italy, and maybe it will help, if only a little. I can't wait to see her face tonight when she sees it.

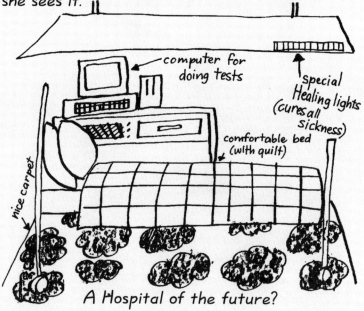

computer for doing tests

special Healing lights (cures all sickness)

comfortable bed (with quilt)

nice carpet

A Hospital of the future?

Lots of things happened at school this week. Carlos fell during a gym class and broke his arm. His face went all white — just like a ghost — and he didn't stop yelling. What bad luck, just after he'd found Thumper in the school vegetable garden, munching on one of Ms. Poulos's prize lettuces! Now Carlos won't be able to perform his magic act anyway.

Juliana won a medal in the inter-school cross-country championships. She's really good at running. I think she's so good she'll end up in the Olympics one day. And the list went up on the bulletin board with all the acts for the concert. Suzie and Sharon got in! And so did Melissa Armitage, the smallest euphonium player ever. I knew she would. It's going to be a fantastic concert. I can't wait – and my program's going to be the best program ever!

Everyone's nearly finished their projects now. Ms. O'Shane has been bringing in weird things all week. Old telephone books, and florists' wire, and cookie cartons. I wish I could see what she's got locked away in that cupboard of hers! But I suppose we'll all just have to wait and see.

Anna

THE Chinchilla School Concert Program

compiled by Anna Reynard

Chinchilla School proudly presents: A Family Concert

Date: Wednesday, May 7
Time: 8:00 p.m. sharp
Place: Chinchilla School Hall

Act One: The CanCan

**Performed by the
Year 6 Dance Class**

Frou Frou, Fifi, Mimi, Gigi, and friends will whisk you off to a French nightclub with their enchanting dancing.

Act Two: Rap – The Cool School

**Performed by Sharon Blenkinsop and
Suzie Sanchez**

Chill out and get down to the Grand Masters of Rap at Cool Chinchilla. Wicked!

⚜ Act Three: Piano Solo ⚜
– The Entertainer (Scott Joplin)

Performed by Nguyen Anh Ngoc

The flashing fingers and fearless fortissimos of our very own piano virtuoso.

⚜ Act Four: Poem – Tragedy ⚜
on the High Seas

Performed by Arnold Shepherd

A heart-felt and stirring rendition,by our famous poet, Arnold.

Act Five: Song and Dance Routine – The Three Little Pigs

Performed by Kylie, Maria, and Vesna

The Big Bad Wolf should watch out!

Act Six: Euphonium Solo – Moon River

Performed by Melissa Armitage

How can someone so small make a sound so big?

INTERMISSION

Act Seven: Drum Solo – Wipe-out!

Performed by Aldo Maranucci

A scintillating start to our stupendous second half!

Act Eight: The Sugarplum Fairy

Performed by Tatania Chikovsky

Be entranced by the magical dancing of Chinchilla's best kept secret.

Act Nine: Gymnastics Display

Performed by Year 5 students

These sporty students will astound
you with their leaping
and bouncing.

This should give you the general idea!

Friday, May 9

Dear Future,

Today is D-Day! The day we bury the time capsule! Everybody has finished their projects and Ms. O'Shane has carefully packed them into the special box. Mine is the last thing to go in, of course, because I'm still writing it! This is the last time I will write to you, dear friends from the future, then I'll pack my journal into the box with the basketball cards and the video and all the other projects, and Ms. O'Shane will seal up everything.

Time Capsule
Do not open for
100 years!!

It's been really good being able to write about how I've felt over the last few weeks. Nonna being so sick made me really sad, but writing about it has made me realise just how special she is to me.

Yesterday we went to visit her in the hospital. She's happier now that she has her sunflower quilt. Nonna looked up at me and gave me a wink. She had good news for us, she said. The doctors told her the operation went very well, so she'll be able to come home soon, maybe as soon as next week!

Mom and I hugged her. Nonna home again next week – what fantastic news! We'll be able to read my book together again, under her sunflower quilt, at home, where Nonna belongs.

So many things have happened in the last few weeks. Like the concert, and being asked to write the program for it. Things that I might forget about if I didn't write them down. Things that I could look back on in twenty years' time (if I'd kept my journal!) and say: "Did I do that?"

So I've made a decision. Tonight, straight after school, I'm going to ask Mrs. Widdershins (she's been baby-sitting for us while Nonna's been in hospital) to take me down to the mall so that I can buy a new book. A leathery brown-covered one, with smooth creamy pages. I'm going to start a whole new journal. Just for me. Maybe I'll keep a journal for the rest of my life. Who knows?

We had the concert on Wednesday night. It was terrific! So many people came. They clapped and cheered all the acts, and laughed when the curtain fell down, right in the middle of Arnold's dramatic hand gestures. He wasn't very happy about that; what a "tragedy" it turned out to be!

I sat out in the audience with my parents and Marco. It was a pity Nonna couldn't have been there. She would have enjoyed it. She loves singing and dancing. At intermission I went backstage to see my friends. They were all laughing and joking, having a great time putting on make-up and costumes. It looked like fun. Maybe next year – if I feel like it – I might write something to recite. Maybe. Perhaps Nonna could help me. I'll ask her tomorrow.

This morning we finally found out what Ms. O'Shane has been doing with all those popsicle sticks and boxes and the sand and green slime. She unlocked her mysterious cupboard and brought out her own special project for the time capsule: a model of the school. It was fantastic! She'd used the box for a base; the wire to make the fence; the green slime to show the fish pond; the sand for the sandpits under the play equipment; and the cookie cartons

Ms. O'Shane

gr
fis

and popsicle sticks for the school buildings.
And she'd made little figures of all of us
out of papier mâché, using the pages from
the telephone books. There we were –
walking around the school! She'd even
made a figure of herself, with her bushy
red hair, standing in the middle of the
playground, flapping her arms. And there
was a little black spider tootling along in
front of her. Amazing.

Well, it's time to stop writing now. I hope you enjoy what our class has put together to show what life was like in our time.

I just wish one thing. I wish I could be there to see the looks on your faces when you open our time capsule, one hundred years from now. Goodbye, and good luck in the future,

Your friend from
    the twentieth century,

Anna

TITLES IN THE SERIES